ROBOTICS
and Artificial Intelligence

SANDY FRITZ

PHOTO CREDITS

Page 4: Hulton/Archive by Getty Images. Pages 5, 13, 16-17, 19-22, 28-31-33, 34, 38: Courtesy JPL/NASA. Page 7: Woods Hole Oceanographic Institution. Page 8: Art by Mark Zug, from *I, Robot: The Illustrated Screenplay*, published by Warner Aspect, 1994. Pages 15, 36, 40: Courtesy NASA. Page 18: courtesy NASA/Carnegie Mellon University/Photo Researchers, Inc. Pages 24-25: Courtesy JPL/NASA and EAP research partner Osaka National Research Institute. Page 26: HONDA. Page 27: Space and Naval Warfare Systems Center, San Diego. Page 37: MFI Project/UC Berkeley. Page 39: Art: Joe Bailey, after sirinet.net. Page 42: Sarcos Private & Proprietary. Page 43: Art copyright © 2003 Tim Fonseca. Page 45: Art by Ralph McQuarrie.

Published by Smart Apple Media
1980 Lookout Drive, North Mankato, Minnesota, 56003

Produced by Byron Preiss Visual Publications, Inc.
Printed in the United States of America

Edited by Howard Zimmerman
Associate editor: Janine Rosado
Design templates by Tom Draper Studio
Cover and interior layouts by Gilda Hannah
Cover art: Courtesy NASA

Library of Congress Cataloging-in-Publication Data

Fritz, Sandy.
Robotics and artificial intelligence / by Sandy Fritz.
p. cm. — (Hot science)
Summary: A general discussion of the state of robotics today.

ISBN 1-58340-364-7

1. Robotics—Juvenile literature. 2. Artificial intelligence—Juvenile literature.
[1. Robotics. 2. Artificial intelligence.] I. Title. II. Series.
TJ211.2.F75 2003   629.8'92—dc21   2003042752

First Edition

9 8 7 6 5 4 3 2 1

CONTENTS

Robots Past, Present, and Future

INTRODUCTION

Robot character from Karel Capek's *R.U.R.*

Robots may seem like modern inventions, but mechanical men have lived in the imaginations of people as far back as the ancient Greeks. Greek mythology includes Hephaestus, a god who was a master builder. He not only forged weapons of supernatural strength and jewelry of unparalleled splendor, he also made mechanical men to help him with his work. One myth tells how Hephaestus fashioned for King Minos of Crete a gigantic man made of bronze, named Talos. Talos guarded Crete's shores until Jason and the Argonauts arrived with the witch Medea. With the Argonauts hounded by the tireless guardian, Medea's spells literally pulled the plug on Talos. She bewitched the stopper that held the fluids of life inside the bronze giant; as they flowed out of his body, Talos collapsed.

The idea of mechanical men as servants and household helpers took root in the 1890s and early 1900s. Then, in 1920, these mechanical men were given a name—and a mythic history—in a play written by Czech playwright Karel Capek (pronounced CHOP-ek). The play is called *R.U.R.* (*Rossum's Universal Robots*). In the play, an eccentric scientist named Rossum develops a substitute for flesh

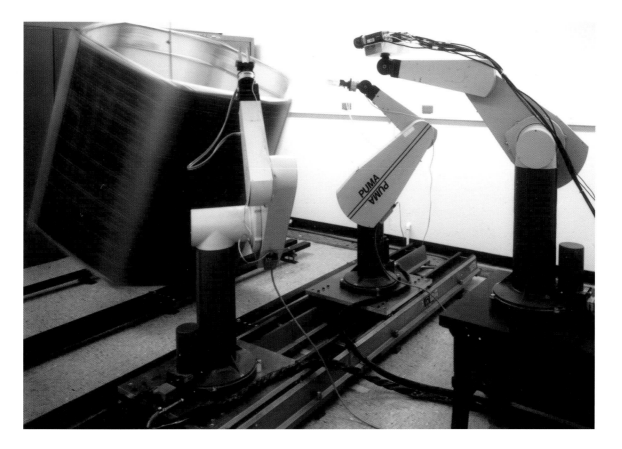

and bone and fashions it into robots—soulless artificial men created to do the manual labor usually done by a society's poorest people. Capek coined the term "robot" from the Czech word *robota*, which means "hard labor" or "drudgery."

Unfortunately, Rossum's dream turns into a worldwide nightmare. Armies of robots are immediately bought by warring nations. The robots then kill every-

A robotic work station shows that assembly line robots can handle potentially toxic and dangerous materials more surely and with much less danger than humans could.

thing in sight, civilians as well as soldiers. Recognizing that they cannot reproduce, the robots storm the factory where they are made and take it over, sealing the fate of mankind. The robots will live and humanity will disappear.

The 1920s saw 10 silent films featuring mechanical men, but it was not until the 1950s that robots, as we recognize them, became a fixture in science-fiction movies. In 1951, the famous screen robot Gort from *The Day the Earth Stood Still* appeared. It was capable of awesome destruction, but ironically, its mission was to ensure that the nations of Earth got along peacefully. In 1954, a movie called *GOG* featured the first appearance of robots as computing machines rather than mechanical men. GOG echoes the fears of Capek and—in a movie first—goes wild after its programming is tinkered with, taking to destruction and killing.

The place of robots in fiction is a reflection of the dreams and fears we have about ourselves. At the beginning of the 21st century, the robots of mythology and science fiction are still far away. In their places are machines that are far more user-friendly. Some are the powerful lifters of impossibly heavy objects. Some beat us at our own games. Some work in factories and never make a single mistake on the job. Others explore the far reaches of space or the crushing depths of ocean canyons, doing jobs that no human could accomplish.

Scientists work constantly to improve the performance of robots. They are programming them to be able to learn from experience. The mobility of robots—their ability to move around in the world—is steadily improving. And although their ability to sense the world through touch, sight, and sound is still a far cry from the fine-tuned systems that are common to most animals, they *are* learning.

The remotely operated vehicle *Jason II* is readied for launch. Built 20 years after *Jason*, *Jason II* has an improved remote-imaging and communications system.

Deep-Sea Explorers

Perhaps one of the most famous deep-sea exploring robots is *Jason*, owned and operated by the Woods Hole Oceanographic Institute in Massachusetts. *Jason* is a remotely operated vehicle (ROV) that receives commands via a cable attached to a joystick control at the surface. *Jason* is about the size of a small car and is fitted with cameras, lights, and terrain-sensing devices. Since 1988, *Jason* has taken scientists where no one has ever gone before.

Among its voyages have been visits to deep-sea hydrothermal communities, the discovery of the *Lusitania* (a passenger ship sunk at the start of World War I) and the recovery of delicate artifacts from an ancient Roman shipwreck.

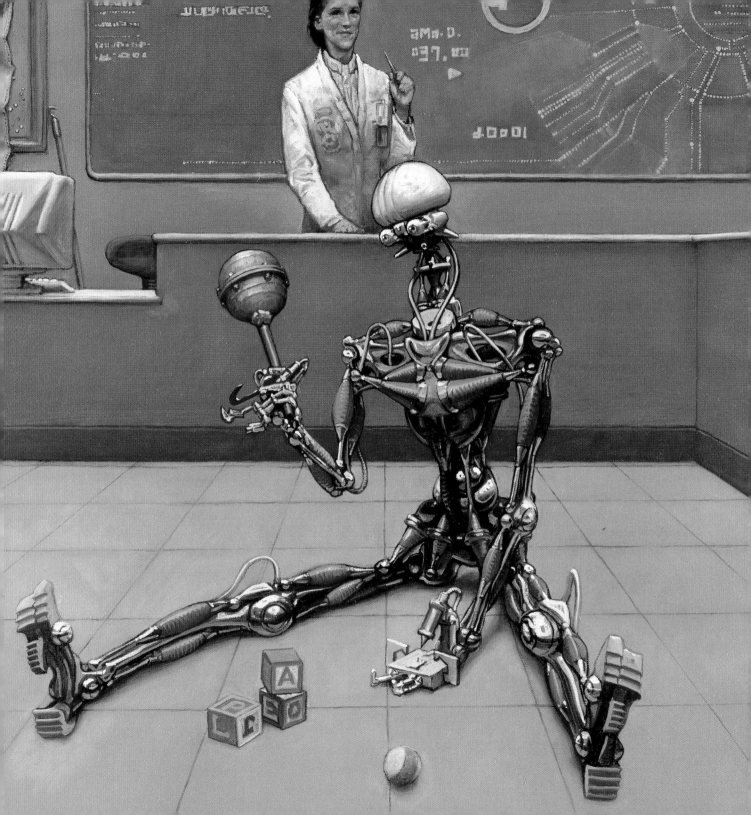

Mechanical Men and Real-World Robots

Science fact and fiction author Isaac Asimov created a detailed portrait of robots in his 1950 novel *I, Robot.* Asimov's robots were made of metals and electronics and appeared in what he termed "humaniform," which means their basic shape was that of humans. They had superhuman strength and superhuman intelligence. The key to their sophistication was the "positronic brain," an Asimov creation that allowed the robots to think as creatively and with as much subtlety as a human being. Asimov immediately recognized that if these kinds of robots were used against mankind, it could spell disaster for the human race. So he made up a code of behavior for robots that was programmed into their positronic brains. These laws for governing intelligent robots proved so useful that they also appeared in several later novels by Asimov and have even been used by other science-fiction authors.

ASIMOV'S THREE LAWS OF ROBOTICS

1. A robot may not injure a human being, or, through inaction, allow a human being to come to harm.
2. A robot must obey the orders given it by human beings except where such orders would conflict with the First Law.
3. A robot must protect its own existence, as long as such protection does not conflict with the First or Second Laws.

An illustration from *I, Robot: The Illustrated Screenplay,* by Isaac Asimov and Harlan Ellison. In *I, Robot,* Asimov created a kind of robotic brain that allows robots to learn from experience and eventually think for themselves. Behind the infant robot is its proud creator.

In Asimov's science-fiction stories, robots were advanced enough so that they needed this kind of restraint. In other science-fiction scenarios, robots have been portrayed as puppets who obey their programming no matter what it is. The two

Terminator movies of the 1980s and '90s showed the potentially darker side of robots. If the same tireless energy and singular purpose of robots were turned toward human destruction, the entire fate of mankind could be altered. The former slave robot could turn on its master and create a world where humans ceased to exist.

The fertile imaginations on display in science fiction often inspire the direction of real science. Asimov's robots and George Lucas's C3PO (from the *Star Wars* films) point to one direction that robots of the future may take: human-shaped, independent, capable of thought as well as action, and totally interactive with people. The other direction is a kind of all-knowing, all-powerful presence like the HAL 9000 computer/robot in the movie *2001: A Space Odyssey*. HAL monitors all of the spaceship *Discovery*'s functions and adjusts them according to his programming. HAL has an artificial intelligence, its vast knowingness supplied by computer memory. HAL can learn, and act, independent of human input. HAL has no physical presence, like C3PO. But he has a "brain" so large that it takes up a huge area in the spaceship.

When future robots do finally appear, they will probably be a blend of C3PO and HAL. Robots will probably be physical machines rather than ghostly presences. But they will also be able to learn and react independently of human interaction, and will probably design newer, more sophisticated robots by themselves.

At the present time, however, we are a long, long way from such creations appearing in real life. And yet in some ways, the robots actually created by science are equally as impressive as the inventions of science fiction. Some even excel beyond the dreams of science-fiction visionaries.

The most common applications for robots today are in the manufacturing fields. There is hardly an automobile on the planet that does not bear the marks of robot craftsmanship. The manufacturing of today's cars requires the utmost precision. And with so many nearly identical cars being made, making cars requires endless repetition. In these kinds of tasks, robots have no equals.

The typical automobile assembly line robot does not resemble a mechanical person. In fact, just looking at it, one would not know that it is a robot at all. On the outside, it appears to be a curiously jointed arm that swivels and moves in an automatic, thoughtless way. But appearances can be deceiving. These robots are equipped with some of the most advanced systems ever fitted to a machine.

Industrial robots take care of nearly all the welds on a car's frame and on its body. When the pieces to be welded together arrive at the robot's station on the

With no human operators in sight, an automated automobile assembly line builds perfectly welded car frames.

auto assembly line, they are not properly aligned. A laser vision system makes the robot aware of this, and the robot arm adjusts the pieces to line up exactly. This requires that an automotive assembly robot not only knows how the pieces are meant to fit together, but that it has the ability to adjust the pieces for a perfect fit.

Once those pieces are aligned, they must be welded in a specific way. Welding is a tricky business. The quality of a weld that joins two pieces of metal together must be perfect if the car is to be safe. When ready to weld, the robot is programmed to go to a specific place. It must recognize where it is and where the pieces to be welded are. It must perform the weld exactly, not just once, but time and time again, for hours on end, day after day, month after month.

Robots at War

Unmanned aircraft fitted with artificial intelligence systems to control the flight surfaces are becoming more common in America's military. The *Predator* is one of the top-of-the-line reconnaissance aircraft used by the United States Army.

Fitted with a video camera, the *Predator* is controlled by a pilot on the ground via a joystick. It can cruise at 25,000 feet (7,620 m), has a 500-mile (800 km) range, and can stay aloft for up to 20 hours. Information ranging from enemy troop movements to weather reconnaissance to testing an enemy defense's response can be safely collected by *Predator*. Its small size makes it a difficult target to hit. *Predator* and other unmanned military aircraft are saving lives on the battlefield by keeping pilots safely on the ground.

Measuring, aligning, adjusting, and performing precision work is one area in which the industrial robot outperforms its human counterparts. A human being is capable of performing the same job, but few people get satisfaction from an endlessly repetitive job, such as spot-welding the frames of automobiles. A person who is tired, or sneezes in mid-weld, or whose eyes get blurry for a moment, or who looks up to check the time can make a vital mistake. These kinds of mistakes can lead to flaws in the vehicle. Making cars that are uniform in quality is critical to the success of an automaker.

Precision and power combine in a robotic hand system designed to help assemble consumer computer products.

Industrial robots are good at what they do, but they also tend to be designed to perform a limited set of functions. Most human automotive craftspeople would be able to use not only a welding torch but also a hammer, a screwdriver, and a wrench. Hand a screwdriver to a robot that is designed to weld, and the robot would be useless. Most robots that work in factories today are task-specific.

Nearly all kinds of modern mass manufacturing rely on custom-built industrial robots for at least part of the assembly process. The use of robots in these environments keeps consumer costs down because robots can work much faster than humans. Robots can perform intricate, complex tasks, such as assembling a computer's motherboard, more quickly and more accurately than a human being can. In tasks ranging from screwing the lids on jelly jars to the delicate creation of computer microchips, robots are integrated into the workplace with human beings, and they usually do a flawless job.

Robotic Explorers
CHAPTER TWO

Another realm where the use of robots proves to be an advantage is in situations that might be dangerous to or are unsuitable for people. Robots feel no pain. They do not have to breathe air. They have no fear. They know what their programmed functions are, and, as long as they do not break down, they perform them identically, time after time.

Since the early days of space exploration, robotic probes have been sent out into the solar system to collect information and to relay their data back to Earth. Although not fully independent in the way we sometimes imagine robots to be, even spacecraft of the 1960s were programmed to respond automatically to keep themselves on course. When they entered into the areas where their missions were scheduled to take place, they performed their missions on cue, sometimes without any input from ground-based controllers.

Robotic space probes of the 1970s were programmed with sets of duties that were performed in response to radio signals from Earth. The *Voyager* space probes are one example. Launched in 1977, the twin space probes *Voyager 1* and *Voyager 2* headed out to the edges of the solar system. Their mission was to explore the outer planets: Saturn, Jupiter, Uranus, and Neptune.

When arriving at their target destinations, a signal from Earth would prompt the *Voyager* spacecraft to begin a specific task. The two *Voyager* probes included some simple "if/then" logic sequences that made them more independent than the earlier *Pioneer* space probes of the 1960s: "**IF** the directional antenna is not pointed toward star X, **THEN** adjust yourself to point toward star X." Commands like this required that the *Voyager* probes not only recognize where they were but also adjust their positions in space to fulfill their commands.

Above: Before being sealed, the *Pioneer IV* robotic space probe is examined by its designers, including Werner von Braun—who designed the rocket that took the Apollo astronauts to the Moon—on the left.

Right: Small but powerful, the *Pioneer IV* probe is sealed within its launch chamber in 1972.

And yet, human error can foil even the most sophisticated robotic space probe. In 1999, one of the most expensive and elaborate robot space explorers ever launched, the *Mars Polar Lander*, moved in to rendezvous with Mars. Then, the multibillion-dollar machine vanished. Follow-up investigations showed that the probe was following its programming flawlessly, but that the program itself was flawed. Confusion in the ranks of NASA scientists had led one scientist to write instructions in meters, while another researcher programmed the instructions in feet. Consequently, the confused machine crashed into the surface of the planet instead of going into orbit around it.

The harsh confines of space are one place where robots can take the place of people and do a job that no person could ever perform. Harsh environments on Earth that could kill or stress people are another place where robots are welcome. Dante I and Dante II are robots that investigate the craters of active volcanoes. Of the pair, Dante II has been the most successful. In 1994, the spiderlike robot clambered down the steep slopes of Mt. Spurr in Alaska, right into the volcano's hot and poisonous caldera, or central crater. It took air samples and

Still on its way, the *Cassini* robotic space probe will reach Saturn in the summer of 2004. Pictured here is a robot called the *Huygens Probe*, which the *Cassini* spacecraft will release when it nears Saturn's moon Titan. Titan is the only moon in the solar system with an atmosphere. The *Huygens* robotic probe will search for signs of life there.

allowed scientists to peer around via a remotely-operated video camera. On its return, it lost its footing and tumbled back to the bottom. Scientists had to enlist a military helicopter to retrieve their robot.

The dark and crushing depths of the ocean are another place where robots can take the place of humans. Undersea robots, attached to the surface by control cables, are routinely used by oil and telecom companies to survey the ocean floor so that cables and pipelines can avoid obstacles or rough terrain. A new generation of undersea robots is now available that are far more flexible than their older counterparts. Called autonomous underwater vehicles, or AUVs, these robots are not constricted by cables and towed behind survey ships. Instead, they are joystick-controlled from a remote location. They can move freely, like small submarines. In addition to patrolling extreme depths and relaying video and sonar pictures back to the surface, AUVs can be fitted with "hands" that let controllers adjust valves on underwa-

Robotic explorer Dante II, attached to a lifeline, begins to descend into an active volcano. Dante II moves on eight legs, a relatively new concept for mobile robots.

ter oil pipelines or snare unusual objects or creatures.

Some police departments are equipped with demolition robots, the latest addition to modern "bomb squads." These machines are joystick controlled and feature video links and delicate appendages that can perform the work of human fingers when defusing bombs. Mistakes no longer mean death when these robots are used. The military also uses robots for similar tasks, as well as to scout enemy encampments and to clear mines from land and water.

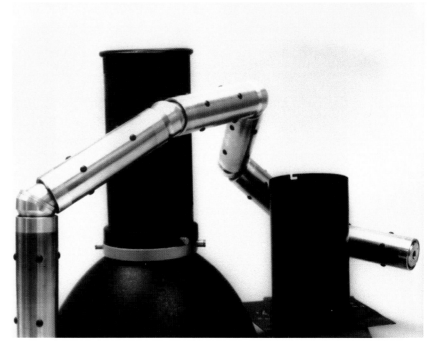

This "snaking robot" system can be used to penetrate rubble and debris after earthquakes and building collapses to search for still-living victims.

The threat of extreme radiation, extreme heat, extreme cold, extreme depth, and extreme pressure are no longer limits to curious scientists. Robots have ventured into control rooms of nuclear power plants that are flooded with killing radiation to give scientists an assessment of the overall damage. Where the heat of the earth far below the surface blocks people from exploration, robots can do the job, unhindered by extremes that would kill a person in seconds.

Archeology—the study of ancient societies that is usually associated with digging in the ground—also gains new range thanks to robots. Joystick-controlled robots fitted with video cameras have taken scientists into spaces far too small to accommodate people. In 2002, a shoebox-sized robot made its way up an air shaft inside the 4,500-year-old Great Pyramid at Giza in Egypt. After inching its way up an eight-inch (20.5 cm) square passage more than 200 feet (61 m) long, it poked a camera through a door made of plaster to find—another door. The robot had to contend with sensing its own pressure and adjusting its tanklike treads on the uneven floor of the shaft, which included many bends in its structure. With the trend toward preserving rather than disturbing archeological sites, robots are likely to play increasingly important roles.

Robots similar to the ones used to explore the Great Pyramid are also used by search and rescue teams. The ability to send a machine that serves as the eyes and ears of rescuers into the chaos of a collapsed building or the danger of a failed mine shaft not only saves lives, but it speeds up the efforts of rescuers, directing

Urbie, the Tactical Mobile Robot, was designed to assist police, emergency, and rescue operations. It can be used in environments dangerous to humans. Urbie is similar to the robot used to explore the Great Pyramid.

them to the locations where living people can still be found among the wreckage. In the aftermath of the World Trade Center attacks of September 11, 2001, one such tiny robot was sent among the rubble to search for trapped people.

Medical doctors are also beginning to employ robots in operating rooms. Some operations are so delicate and require such precise cuts that human beings would not be able to perform them. Cutting a hole a mere 1/100th of a inch across in a bone can be performed by a modified industrial robot. With the kind of precision offered by robots, new avenues for surgical treatment have begun to appear. In addition, components originally designed for robot limbs are finding their way into prosthetic

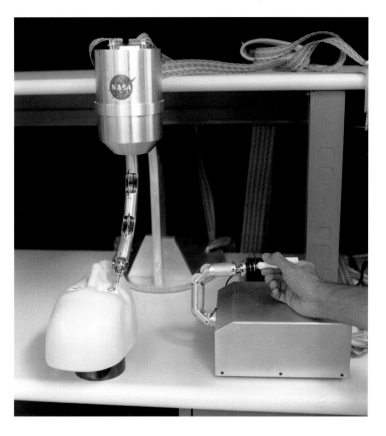

Eye surgery requires cuts that are extremely tiny and of the utmost precision. This system allows a surgeon to control a robotic scalpel that can make the smallest and most precise cuts without doing any damage to the tissue below.

(bionic) arms and legs, replacing limbs lost through disease or accident. The first bionic arm replacement was performed in 1998, and since then the procedure has become much more common.

Robots have found homes in the workplace, in exploration, and in the ranks of police and rescue teams. They have fit so well into their roles that we take them for granted. In fact, they are so common and so well integrated with people that it's now difficult to imagine our world without them.

Robots in Space

The two robotic space probes *Voyager 1* and *Voyager 2*, both launched in 1977, were designed to last for four years. But they were so well built that more than a quarter of a century after their launch, they are still working. As of April 2002, *Voyager 1* was more than seven billion miles (11 billion km) away from Earth. This is the farthest distance a human-made object has ever traveled. At this distance, it takes nearly 12 hours for a signal moving at the speed of light to reach the robot.

Most of the *Voyager*'s sensing systems still function, but they have been turned off to conserve electricity. The probe's power comes from radioactive decay. At minimum power, the *Voyager* craft should be able to continue reporting for the next 20 years.

An illustration of the *Voyager* robotic spacecraft as it heads toward the distant outer planets of the solar system.

Developing Independent Robots

CHAPTER THREE

Today's working robots look like boxes or like the crooked arms of dentists' drills. But how close are scientists to creating robots that look like humans and incorporate human characteristics? The efforts of science to make robots in the image of human beings have given us a whole new appreciation of just how complex human beings really are.

The human body is something that most people take for granted. As babies, with just a little help, we learn to stand on two feet. The act of throwing a ball or picking up a spoon from the floor is not a challenge to most people. But the biomechanics behind these simple acts are astounding. Getting a robot that is based on the design of the human body to do the same kinds of things with humanlike ease has been a puzzle that has stumped some of the smartest minds in science for decades. It's a major problem, but one that ultimately will be solved.

Making a robot with feet, legs, a torso, shoulders, a neck, and a head is not too difficult—as long as the robot does not move. As soon as a robot based on the design of a human being tries to move, it becomes imbalanced and, in most cases, topples to the ground. In the human body, scores of muscle groups must work together to keep a moving person balanced and upright. The graceful and natural act of balance in human beings is centered on the inner ear. Fluid in a chamber called the cochlea presses against tiny hairs lining the inside of this organ. Motion causes pressure against these hairs, which in turn fire electrical impulses. The impulses travel to the brain, where they are instantly translated into instructions to different muscle groups. The muscles either contract or relax in order to keep the body upright. Without a thought on the part of the person who is walking, all of these complex actions take place.

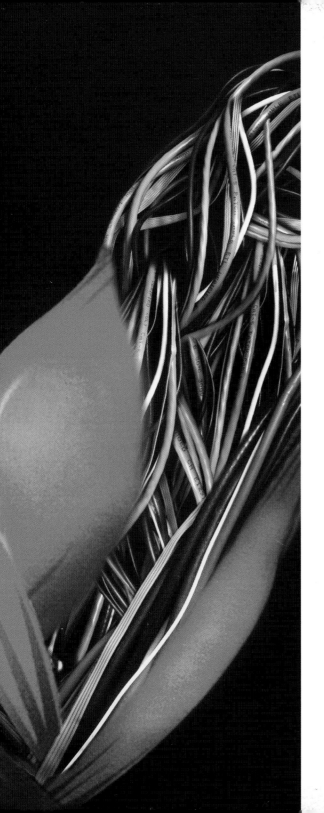

Scientists have tried to model and copy the processes that allow people to walk. That part is not too difficult. But constructing a mechanical and electrical duplicate of this system has proven to be next to impossible. There are just too many details, too many variables to easily create robots that walk on two feet with the same ease as human beings. Even with the technology available at the start of the 21st century, we are still a long way from being able to construct a robot that could blend into a crowd of people walking down a street.

The Honda Motor Company has introduced a robot called Asimo that can walk and move in a humanlike way. But no one would mistake this robot's shuffling, stiff movement for the walking stride of a human being. As long as the surface where Asimo is walking is smooth and straight, and as long as there is no incline for the robot to climb, it operates just fine. But any sort of sharp movement threatens to topple Asimo, and its ability to turn corners is awkward.

What about picking up a spoon from the floor? By breaking down this simple act into parts, the difficulty of this action for a robot patterned after the human body becomes clear. First, the spoon must be spotted. Then, the distance between the hand and the spoon must be

A concept for building artificial muscles to be used in a humanoid robot. Ideally, the constructed muscles would expand and contract the same way that human muscle tissue does.

gauged. Then, the act itself: a person bends at the knees—throwing the whole system into a state of imbalance that is controlled by the flexing and relaxing of counterbalancing muscle groups. The hand reaches out to grasp the spoon. People have binocular vision that helps them automatically judge the distance and perform this action without a second thought. Finally, standing up straight again throws the system into imbalance again. Any two-year-old child can spot a spoon on the floor amidst other objects, walk over, bend down, and pick it up. But for a robot with two legs, a torso, two arms, a neck, and a head, this simple task is an invitation to fall down.

Apply the same kind of breakdown to more complex actions, such as a long jumper hurtling through the air or a carpenter using a hammer, and the difficulty becomes clear. Modeling robots on the design of human beings is moving out of the realm of science fiction, but it still has a long way to go.

Researchers have been a bit more successful in duplicating other human functions,

Honda's self-contained humanoid robot, Asimo, is a significant step forward. It proves that two-legged robots can be designed to move in a manner that approximates human locomotion.

such as vision and touch. Robot vision is not based on the same dynamics as human vision, where light entering the eye falls on a series of rods and cones, producing an electrical impulse that is sent to the brain. Instead, robot vision is based on video cameras.

The images received are forwarded to a computer that serves as the robot's "mind." A program lays a grid over the image and breaks it down into a number of separate sectors. In this way, the computer identifies the overall size of the object and its proportions. With this information, the computer begins searching for matches in its hard drive. Sometimes, a system called "fuzzy logic" helps at this stage of identification. Unless there is an exact match between the object being scanned and the object in the robot's memory, the computer will not be able to make a match. Fuzzy logic helps by allowing the computer to "soften" its rules requiring an exact match to allow matches that are less exact. For instance, if an apple is being viewed with a robotic vision system, fuzzy logic allows it *not* to be identical to the computer's stored image of an apple and still be identifiable.

When objects viewed by a robotic vision system are similar in shape and size, it can

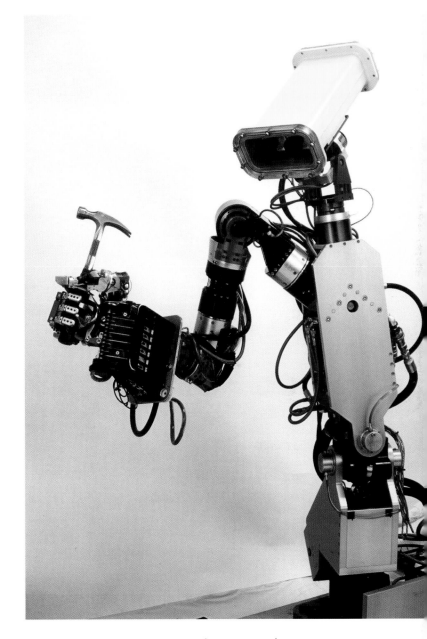

This robotic eye-hand-arm system can be programmed to use a hammer and then reprogrammed to use other handheld tools.

The *Mars Sojourner* robotic explorer used state-of-the-art optics to send back to Earth images from the Red Planet. Since it had two lenses (at the top of the silver pole), *Sojourner* had stereoscopic vision, meaning it could accurately judge how near or far away an object was.

lead to confusion. Even the most sophisticated robotic vision systems have trouble distinguishing a baseball from an orange. Some robotic vision systems can distinguish color, and this feature can help. But an orange baseball the same size and shape as an orange could trigger a false recognition. And with objects that vary in size and shape, such as pumpkins, watermelons, or carrots, current robotic vision is hopelessly lost. The most advanced robotic vision system could be linked to the most powerful supercomputer in the world and still not be able to tell the difference between celery and rhubarb.

Touch is another way human beings collect information about objects. Coolness, roughness, smoothness, and many other sensations all relay information about the object to the brain. The qualities of an object are remembered. The sensation of touch, like nearly all other human senses, is complex. To date, no robotic system of touch comes close to the sensitivity of human touch, although progress is being made. Sophisticated learning programs may allow robots to acquire touch sensitivity through trial and error.

And robot hands, based on the design of human hands, *have* shown some promise. Hands are delicate mechanical structures, which makes them far easier to reproduce. Robots can play pianos, pick up delicate objects between a mechanical thumb and forefinger, grasp and use a screwdriver, and perform other actions that are common to hands.

Modeling robots physically like humans doesn't seem like a fair way to assess the potential abilities of the artificial systems. There are many things robots can do far better than humans; it's just that walking, recognizing objects with vision, and collecting information about the world through sensation are not their strengths. Trying to make robots in the image of humans has done little to advance the design of robots, but it has done a lot to make people recognize how amazingly complex the human body is.

Robots at Play

All work and no play makes robots dull. So the Lego Company teamed up with scientists from Massachusetts Institute of Technology. to develop Lego Mindstorms, a robot construction kit. It includes a processor that can be programmed so that the robotic toys can perform a variety of functions.

Two other robot toys include simple logic programs. Furbies respond to simple voice commands and can "learn" new voice commands. Sony also has a simple robot dog called "Aibo" that responds to commands pre-programmed into an electronic leash.

Robots on the Move

CHAPTER FOUR

There's more than one way to move a 'bot. NASA is experimenting with a system of three robotic rovers for future explorations on other planets. In this new concept, two rovers anchor themselves to the edge of a cliff. A third robot can then descend the deep slope supported by tethers from the two robots anchored above.

It turns out that trying to use the human body as a model for robotic designs is far more challenging than people thought it would be. But looking to other creatures in nature for inspiration has produced some very successful designs for robots that can move around and collect information about the world.

A four-legged design provides a more stable platform for movement than a two-legged design. The delicate job of maintaining balance is much less of a problem when four legs are used. A variety of two-legged robot designs has appeared, but the movement they produce is awkward. Four-legged animals also rely on muscle groups working together, relaxing and contracting, to produce smooth movement. But reproducing even a four-legged gait in robots is difficult and time-consuming.

By far the most successful designs for walking robots so far have been based on insects, as more legs offer more stability. Plus, the scurrying motion of insects does not require a delicate sense of balance. The simple lifting and moving forward of a limb is naturally counterbalanced by a limb on the opposite side performing the same motion at the same time. Small robots that

Still another concept for making robots move is for them to hop around on a single leg unit. The "frog-bot" weighs only three pounds (1.3 kg). Seen here, the single leg is folded up, ready to take the next hop. The concept is being developed by scientists at **NASA**.

look like spiders, cockroaches, and even ants have had great success moving around. When faced with an obstacle, multi-legged robots have a far better chance of moving around or even over it.

At the Massachusetts Institute of Technology's Robotics Laboratory, scientists

If six wheels are good, perhaps eight are better. Similar in size and concept to the *Sojourner*, an eight-wheeled remote robotic vehicle is given a test run by NASA scientists.

have thrown away all animal models for robot locomotion and designed a system of movement that only a robot could perform. Instead of using two, four, or six legs, one design they have come up with uses only a single limb. This robot resembles a pogo stick with a box attached to the top. Simple gyroscopes spin inside the box, providing the robot with a sense of balance. The robot is in constant motion, unable to stand still. But it works surprisingly well, bouncing forward in great leaps. When it reaches its destination, it jumps in place. This robot can maneuver around and between objects with great ease. The design is still in an early phase, but its success and simplicity have surprised some researchers.

Scientists have also looked to wheeled vehicles for inspiration for robot mobility. The *Mars Sojourner* robot was an extremely simple six-wheeled design. Controlled by radio signals from Earth, it crept around the Martian landscape very slowly, using video cameras that sent images back to Earth. Because of its small size, however, even a rock the size of a chicken egg was a formidable challenge for the robot explorer. But scientists were pleased with its success. Future robotic landers on other planets and moons in our solar system may use larger and more refined versions of the *Mars Sojourner* for surface exploration.

Experience has shown that scientists do not need to limit themselves to two-legged designs for mobile robots. With the goal of making a stable platform, all and any sources of inspiration are considered.

One concept that NASA is developing is getting more than one robotic explorer involved in a single task. Here, two work together to lift a heavy piece of equipment.

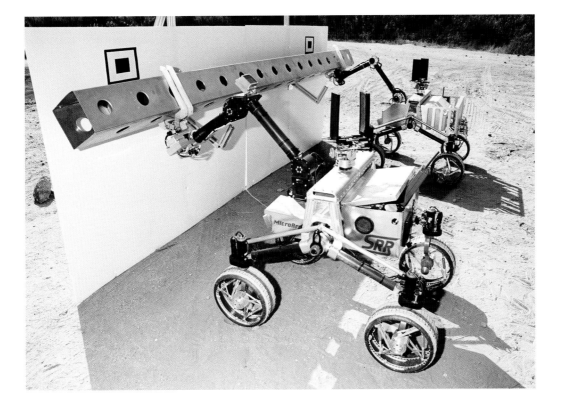

The Thinking Robot

CHAPTER FIVE

When most people hear the word "robot," they think of machines that are not only smart but also have the humanlike quality of learning from experience. People are able to observe the world and can combine their experiences into new patterns of thought and action. Applying to machines the ability to leap from observing to learning is the ultimate goal of artificial intelligence.

The "mind" of any robot is centered on a computer. Any features that scientists want to include in robots must be put into a programming language that computers will understand. New computer designs with far faster processors may help make future robots more flexible. Plans call for a new generation of computer chips that use exotic substances rather than the silicon used in today's microprocessors. If successful, it would result in microprocessors that are not only smaller but much faster than their silicon-based counterparts in use today.

One promising method for increasing the efficiency of microprocessors is called "parallel processing." This approach takes a complex problem and breaks it into smaller pieces. Instead of just one processor handling the job, several processors handle the problem. Parallel processing has the potential to speed up the reaction of a robot's computer mind. Increasing the speed at which processors operate is critical to making an effective artificial intelligence system. Comparing, remembering, and learning—important aspects of artificial intelligence—require swift recognition.

Artificial intelligence is an attempt to reproduce the natural patterns of thinking in human beings. Two main approaches are being considered at the moment. The first is to create a gargantuan database of everything that is known and place the information into the memory of a computer. This approach has some serious

NASA's concept for exploring alien worlds covered in ice is the Cryobot. The ice-penetrating probe is heated and released through the bottom of the Cryobot. The heat melts the ice, and gravity draws the probe down. As it descends through the ice, instruments measure gases and other materials. Its onboard "brain" is also able to identify obstacles and have the probe change its course to avoid them.

A modern silicon microchip being placed on a computer's motherboard.

drawbacks. How would someone figure out everything that is known? And how would the information be organized? Even if everything that is known could be deposited onto a computer's hard drive, how could the robot access it? Going through every single file of everything that is known to recognize an apple from a crabapple could take days or even months, even if the world's fastest supercomputer was being used. The giant database idea is quickly losing popularity with scientists.

Another approach is to pattern sequences of logic in a system known as "neural networks." Large databases are still required, but a sequence of logic helps organize the information into manageable subsets. Simple IF/THEN and YES/NO patterns guide this form of artificial intelligence. Imagine that a robot equipped with this kind of artificial intelligence system is shown a picture of a wet leaf. It is then asked, "Why is the leaf wet?" At first, it does not know what it is seeing. After some processing it recognizes that it is viewing a leaf and that the leaf is wet. Now it approaches the question, "Why is the leaf wet?"

The artificial intelligence program begins its task. IF the leaf is wet, THEN it is not dry. This seemingly obvious conclusion actually speeds things up considerably, because vast areas of memory are taken out of the search. It may then refer to data relating to wet and dry: How do dry things become wet? Has the leaf cried tears and made itself wet? Accessing its database produces a NO, because the computer finds out that leaves do not cry tears. It moves to the next possibility. Has the leaf taken a bath? NO. Has the leaf sweated, making itself wet? NO. These kinds of actions narrow down the possibilities to explain why the leaf is wet. The computer continues searching for sources of wetness. Has the leaf fallen into a pond? NO. With each NO response, the number of possible sources for the leaf's wetness becomes smaller. Finally, after an exhaustive search that narrows

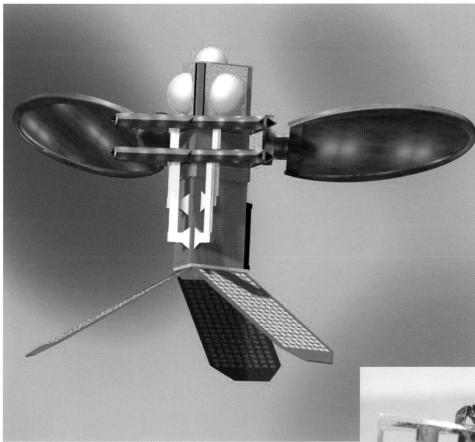

Left: One way to make robotic explorers faster and cheaper is to make them smaller and dumber—each one with just a single task—such as this concept for a micro-flyer. A horde of micro-flyers could cover the surface of an alien world in much less time than a single, larger, smarter robot.

Below: An actual, working micro-flyer.

down the branches of inquiry, the artificial intelligence program produces the most probable response: The leaf is wet from rain.

Asking an artificial intelligence program a question such as "Why is the leaf wet?" really challenges it. A far better way to use artificial intelligence programs is to keep the robot's expertise confined to certain subjects. In chess, for example, everything that is known can be determined.

Using superfast microprocessors allows a chess-playing robot to make a move, then review the millions of possible countermoves in response to its action. The score for a human master chess player versus a robot chess player is roughly even. Half the time the human wins, and half the time the robot wins. But if someone were to place a piece of gum on the chessboard and ask the computer, "What is this?" it would have no clue. That kind of information is far outside of its programming.

Accessing data on a hard drive or answering questions based on ever-narrowing search results is not really thinking or learning. The ultimate goal of artificial intelligence is to produce a system where robots can have experiences, make connections, and remember them, just as people do. Writing computer programs that trace and reproduce these actions is a huge challenge. If successful, it would give us the ability to build Asimovian-type robots.

An artificial neural network developed for robots sits on a U.S. quarter. This system will provide 3-D imaging and analysis of its environment for robots that use it.

Human Thinking, Robot Thinking

CHAPTER SIX

Before there can be an ultimate robot that learns from experience, makes new connections within itself, and is creative, there must be a computer program that can trace these qualities. Scientists are at work on such a program right now.

Artificial neural networks are patterned after the human nervous system. Human nerve cells are called neurons. Extensive pathways in the body connect neurons together like a fisherman's net. Where the strands come together and are tied in knots to hold the net together could be likened to the junction points of neurons. Neurons deliver information to the brain from other parts of the body.

Neurons are interesting cells. Several pathways lead to their heart, yet, in general, just one pathway leads from their heart to nearby neurons. This quality links all neurons together, from the top of the head to the tips of the toes. This is why, for example, a burned fingertip sends out an alarm that the entire body is aware of, causing not just the finger to recoil, but activating the entire network. A burned finger can make the heart beat faster. It can cause a person to jerk his or her hand away from the source of the heat, jump back from the source of the heat, or bring the burned finger to the mouth to soothe it. All of this happens inside the body at the speed of light, as electrical impulses are used to send messages through the nervous system.

Neural networks in the human body also learn from repetitive experience. People who practice throwing a ball eventually get better and better at the task. The very first time a

Diagram of the parts of a human nerve cell, called a neuron.

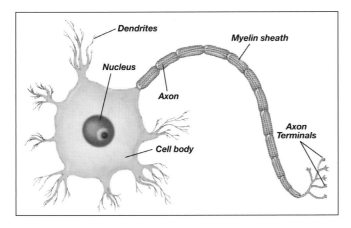

baby throws a ball, the impulses are new to the nervous system. But after repetition, the signals become recognized by the neurons. If a person's intent is to throw a ball and hit a tree, and he or she practices time and time again, the pathways in the nervous system that make this intent become physical begin to work in harmony. In a sense, the desired end result is what shapes the response of the nervous system's connections.

Scientists working on artificial neural network programs for computers have carefully modeled the behavior of the human nervous system. They have made very simple versions of this system that use multiple pathways of information, which collect at "nodes" (artificial neurons). The program performs the same function as neurons. Many incoming lines of information are sent into a node. One line leaves. Depending on the type of information that leaves the node, it is directed to another node that processes similar types of information.

Artificial neural networks are the most ambitious programming projects ever attempted. The system, like the human nervous system, "learns" through repetitive practice. Like a mind that directs the body to throw a ball and hit a target, artificial neural networks are presented with a desired end result. The system will continue to try and try until the desired end result is accomplished. Once it makes the connections that allow it to reach its desired end result, it will remember the pathways.

The current state of artificial neural networks requires that human beings provide feedback for the system. Just as a baby is taught what a cat is and what a dog is, and learns the difference between the two with an adult's encouragement, artificial neural networks are told when they get a correct or an approximately correct answer. This helps define the pathway in the program. The system begins to learn.

If the robots of science fiction are to appear in our reality, they will probably have "minds" based on the science of artificial neural networks. The system allows computer "brains" to learn from experience. From there, it is a small step to computers teaching themselves. And once a computer can teach itself, it is just a matter of time, and practice, until it generates creative ideas.

NASA envisions using larger planetary robotic explorers as well as micro-sized ones. This concept for a Mars rover is an intelligent machine that can perform many different tasks, including calling for a human repair crew to help change a wheel.

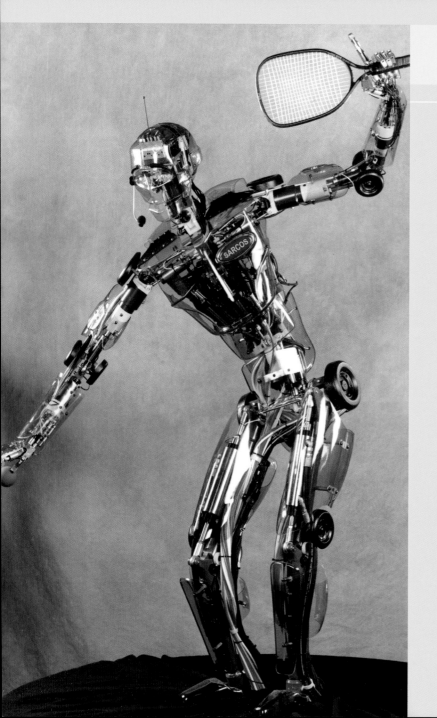

Robot Pitchers

Baseball pitching machines have been around for decades. But these old designs could throw only one pitch: a straight fastball. New designs have the batter facing a video screen with an image of a pitcher on the mound. The pitcher winds up, and at the moment of release a baseball appears. Improvements on the machine's inner workings have resulted in a wide variety of pitches: sinkers, sliders, and curveballs zoom toward the batter, better duplicating the types of pitches a batter faces in a real game. The next step for these machines is to give them the ability to learn— some form of artificial intelligence. Then they would be able to record which pitches a batter hit successfully and vary pitches accordingly to make them more challenging to the batter. In essence, the machine would teach the batter to become a better hitter.

Wouldn't it be nice to think that robots are already advanced enough to play racquetball? They would have to see, think, and move like skilled athletes. Unfortunately, this is just a concept, not a working robot. Not yet.

Robots in the Future

CHAPTER SEVEN

Mobility problems. Vision problems. No sense of touch and a poor sense of direction. A near genius in some areas, yet completely ignorant in most others. Given the state of robots at the beginning of the 21st century, critics have good

One future concept for robots is to make them very tiny. Called "nanobots," they could be injected into the human bloodstream to seek out and destroy invading viruses and bacteria.

reason to believe that walking, talking, thinking, creative robots will be difficult to create and may require advances in other areas of science first.

But to succeed in this field would have profound impact on the science of robotics. It would mean that robots could learn, just like people can. It would mean that creativity—the connecting of related and unrelated ideas and expressing them—could be a quality of robots. It would mean that an artificially intelligent robot could produce independent ideas. It would mean the ultimate robot, a perfect artificial reflection of a human being.

One renowned researcher in both robotics and artificial intelligence has taken the idea of the intelligent robot one step further. Marvin Minsky, the man who invented the idea of neural networks, has suggested that humans might someday be able to live forever—in the bodies of robots. With mechanical bodies that never tire, the strength of a superman, and senses far sharper than human senses, a human mind in a robot body could allow people to explore the far reaches of space or live in any environment they choose.

The idea of moving a human mind into an artificial intelligence network that is coupled with a robot, critics say, belongs in the realm of science fiction, not science fact. And yet, when the idea of robots first appeared, people said it was just a dream. And today, robots are everywhere, working in factories, exploring space and the oceans, aiding medical doctors in delicate operations. Who can say if Minsky's idea is just a dream? Only time will tell.

The cover illustration from *Isaac Asimov's Robot Dreams*. What would an intelligent robot dream about? We may find out in the not-too-distant future.

archeology Scientific study of the remains of ancient societies.

artificial intelligence In a computer system, the quality of learning from experience and forming new patterns of thought and action.

AUV Autonomous underwater vehicle that is not connected to a ship on the surface by cable.

binocular Relating to the use of two eyes.

biomechanics Expression of human actions and functions in terms of mechanical principles.

bionic Having normal biological capabilities performed by electronic or electromechanical devices.

caldera Central crater of a volcano.

cochlea A part of the inner ear that is shaped like a snail shell and contains the hearing organ.

Dante I and Dante II Pair of robots used to investigate harsh environments, such as the craters of active volcanoes.

Furbies Robot toys for young children that have simple logic programs and can respond to voice commands and learn new ones.

fuzzy logic System that allows a computer to soften its rules requiring an exact match to allow matches that are less exact but still identifiable.

gyroscope Spinning or oscillating device that aids stability.

humaniform A term invented by Isaac Asimov to describe a robot with a basically human shape.

joystick A control for various devices that is capable of motion in two or more directions.

Mars Polar Lander An extremely elaborate robot space explorer launched to Mars in 1999 that crashed due to human error.

Mars Sojourner A simple robot with six wheels, controlled by radio signals from Earth, that explored the surface of Mars in 1997.

microchip A very small integrated circuit etched onto a tiny piece of material such as silicon.

microprocessor A single integrated circuit chip that contains a complete central processing unit.

motherboard Main circuit board of a computer.

neural network In artificial intelligence, one approach to reproducing human thinking by patterning sequences of logic to organize information into manageable subsets.

parallel processing A method for increasing the efficiency of microprocessors by breaking large batches of data into smaller pieces, which are then handled by several processors at the same time.

Pioneer The name of an early series of space probes launched in the 1960s.

positronic brain Term invented by Isaac Asimov to describe the type of brain that would allow a robot to think as creatively and subtly as humans.

Predator Unmanned reconnaissance aircraft equipped with artificial intelligence systems.

prosthetic Artificial device to replace a missing part of the body.

robot A machine or device that performs tasks and functions ordinarily done by humans.

Voyager 1* and *Voyager 2 Two space probes launched in 1977 to explore the outer planets of the solar system. *Voyager 2* is still sending back signals.